Today WomWom is going to explore. She digs in the soil to make a burrow. She can see small plants growing in the soil.

There is lots of soil in the garden. The soil in the garden is good for growing plants. Plants get food from the soil.

Good soil can grow good plants.
The roots of the plants can
grow deep in the soil.
WomWom eats the vegetables
in the garden.

WomWom leaves the garden.
She goes to the beach. There is
a lot of sand on the beach.

Vegetables do not grow on the beach. The sand on the beach is too salty. Vegetables need food from the soil to grow.

WomWom returns to the garden. The soil has dead plants, rocks and roots. Dead plants break down to make plant food.

WomWom digs in the soil.
WomWom can see roots of
plants and some earthworms.
Plants get their food and water
from the soil. The water in the
soil comes from the clouds.

WomWom is hungry again.
She walks in the garden. There
is a carrot on the grass. Yum!

Grasses and other plants grow in the soil. WomWom likes eating the leaves and roots of grasses.

WomWom is digging in the soil.
WomWom can find rocks in the
soil. Rocks can break down and
become smaller rocks. Smaller
rocks can break down and
become soil.

Heavy rain can wash the soil
into rivers. Wind can blow soil
away. If the soil washes away
then the plants will have
nowhere to grow.

WomWom sees the machine moving rocks. It will make a wall to protect the side of the river.